No AR test
as of 9/16/17

5/19/98

SPEAKING UP, SPEAKING OUT

SpEaKiNg Up, SpEaKiNg OuT

A Kid's Guide to Making Speeches, Oral Reports, and Conversation

Steven Otfinoski
Illustrated by Carol Nicklaus

The Millbrook Press ■ *Brookfield, Connecticut*

Library of Congress Cataloging-in-Publication Data
Otfinoski, Steven.
Speaking up, speaking out : a kid's guide to making speeches, oral
reports, and conversation / Steven Otfinoski. — Millbrook Press
library ed.
p.   cm.
Includes bibliographical references and index.
Summary: Provides strategies and encouraging tips for speaking in
social situations, reading aloud, presenting oral reports, and making
speeches of all kinds.
ISBN 1-56294-345-6 (lib.bdg.) ISBN 0-7613-0138-0 (pbk.)
1. Public speaking—Juvenile literature. [1. Public speaking.] I. Title.
PN4121.0838   1996
808.5'1—dc20   96-509   CIP   AC

Published by The Millbrook Press, Inc.
2 Old New Milford Road, Brookfield, Connecticut 06804

*To the fifth- and sixth-grade students in the Advanced
Learning Program (ALP) at Stratford Academy,
Stratford, Connecticut, and their dedicated teachers:
Richard Bracci, Betty Mays, Sharon Orsini, and
Michelle Stolzenberg, whose cooperation and help
have been invaluable.*

CoNTENTs

KIDS SPEAK OUT: ON PUBLIC SPEAKING

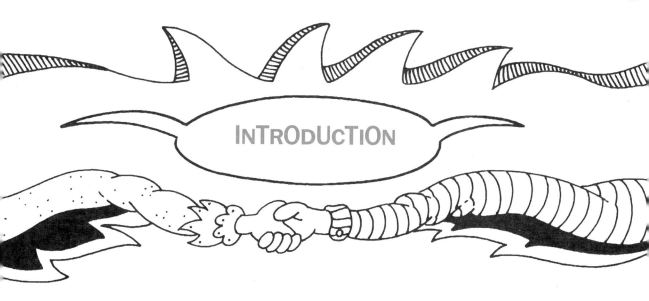

INTRODUCTION

We all speak to other people every day of our lives—to our family, our friends, our teachers, and complete strangers. Speaking for most of us is as natural as breathing. But public speaking often comes less naturally. Public speaking takes place whenever you talk to a group of people in a public setting—a classroom, an auditorium, a dinner gathering—for a particular purpose. That purpose may be to inform, to persuade, or to entertain your audience. When you speak publicly you are talking *to* other people and not with them. For the duration of the time you are speaking, the spotlight is on you. That's both exciting and a little scary.

Most adults aren't that comfortable speaking in public. They'd rather have someone else do it. You probably would, too. But as a student, you will find yourself having to speak to the class on numerous occasions. You will have to, if you haven't already, deliver an oral report or explain how something is done, whether it be making peanut butter cookies or conducting a science experiment.

You may get the urge to run for student council or class president and have to make a campaign speech to the student body. Or you may be given a special award from your youth group and have to give a brief acceptance speech. Even if, by some miracle, you don't have to do any of these things, you will be called on in class to answer a question or read a passage from a textbook. *That's* public speaking, too.

Social speaking is related to public speaking, but there are some differences. Social speaking doesn't mean just "chewing the fat" with your friends; it is talking to people at social functions, such as a party, on the telephone, or in some formal situation, such as when introducing people to each other.

You might ask yourself, "Why should I have to speak in public if I don't want to?" The answer is simple. Public speaking is an important skill that allows you to communicate your thoughts and ideas to other people. This skill will be important not only in your years in school but when you become an adult. Knowledge is power, but the ability to communicate that knowledge is an equally important source of power. Speaking well in public can give you the confidence and ability to succeed in whatever career you choose. It will help make you a leader instead of a follower. There's no better time to start working on your speaking skills than right now.

This guide will point out the different kinds of speaking you may experience as a young person at school, in your social life, and on other special occasions. It will give you advice and suggestions on how to prepare and deliver oral reports, presentations, and speeches successfully. It will help you with reading aloud and talking in social situations, and will improve your telephone skills. Along the way, you'll hear what other kids your age have to say about speaking up and speaking out. In the end, you not only will become better at expressing yourself in words but will actually enjoy it.

CHAPTER ONE
SPEAKING IN
SOCIAL SITUATIONS

Talking to people at parties, on the phone, and in other social situations requires certain skills. Although social speaking is not the same as public speaking—speaking in front of an audience—it will prepare you for public speaking. Social situations are usually less threatening, and success in dealing with them can help you build up your confidence. Many adults and young people often feel awkward or uncomfortable talking to others, especially people they don't know. In this chapter, we will try to help you to overcome this awkwardness and develop the ability to communicate and listen.

INTRODUCING PEOPLE TO EACH OTHER

It's a common situation: You're walking along with a friend and you meet another friend, who doesn't know the person you're with. As the person who knows both people, it's up to you to introduce them to each other. If you don't, it's considered rude—especially to the person you are with. Many people aren't sure how to make introductions, and they get so nervous that they may even forget the name of one friend or the other. Introducing people shouldn't be a cause for panic. Once you know the rules, it will come naturally.

Always first introduce the person you have just met to the person you are already with. Then reverse the introduction:

"John [person you are with], I'd like you to meet Linda Thompson. Linda, John Toro."

If there is more than one person in either group, make sure you include everyone in the introduction.

"John, I'd like you to meet Linda Thompson and Sara Kowalski. Linda and Sara, John Toro."

or

"John and Terry, I'd like you to meet Linda Thompson. Linda, John Toro, and Terry Peters."

Always include the person you're with in your conversation with the person you've just met. Leaving out the person is just as rude as not introducing him or her. If you are on your way somewhere with the person you're with, don't linger too long with the new acquaintance. Your first responsibility is to the friend you are with.

PARTY TALK: THE HOST

It's fun to throw a party, but as the host or hostess, you have certain responsibilities. It is not only your job to see that everyone has enough to eat and drink, but that they also have a good time. Ideally, you should greet each of your guests as they arrive, say a few words, point out where they can find the refreshments, and start them in conversation with another guest, possibly someone they don't know. Once these two people

are talking, you should look for another guest to talk to. Being a good host is a skill that comes with practice and experience. It is a skill that you will need as an adult, and it's a good idea to learn it now.

When the party is ending and guests are beginning to leave, make sure you say goodbye to each of them, thank them for coming, and see that they have whatever they came with—coat, hat, games, CDs, or the dish they brought food in.

PARTY TALK: THE GUEST

As a party guest, you should try to meet and talk to as many people as possible. Although the temptation is to spend all your time with your closest friends, make an effort to talk to any people you don't know very well, and particularly to guests who might not know anyone else there. You just might make a new friend.

Ending one conversation to talk to someone else is a problem that many people face at parties and during other social events. How do you end the conversation without being rude? Here are some ideas for tactful ways you might end a conversation with someone at a party:

"Excuse me, but I see a good friend I need to talk to. I'll see you later."

"I think I'll get something to eat. Is there anything I can get for you?"

"It was nice talking to you. Maybe we can talk again later."

Before you leave the party, make sure you find the person or persons who are giving the party and thank them for inviting you. If you had a good time, be sure to tell them. It'll make them feel good and might just get you invited to their next party!

TALKING ON THE TELEPHONE

Most of us feel very comfortable talking to our friends on the telephone. Every parent who's waited to use the phone while his son or daughter is talking knows that! You might not feel as comfortable, however, when talking to someone's parents, a stranger, or even an answering machine. In these situations, many people get nervous, tongue-tied, and awkward.

Let's review some different types of "formal" phone conversations, starting with you as the caller.

❏ WHEN SOMEONE ELSE ANSWERS

How many times have you called a friend and someone else has answered the phone? What do you say? Here are two examples, one wrong and one right.

WRONG RESPONSE: "Who's this?" (Extremely rude! The person's response will probably be "Who's *this?*")

RIGHT RESPONSE: "This is Bill. Is Ralph there?" (The caller knows at once who you are and whom you want to speak to.)

If you recognize the voice of the person who answers, you should let him or her know.

"Hello, Mr. Alvarez. This is Bill. Is Ralph there?

If your friend isn't home, say that you will call back later or leave a message for your friend. Thank the person before you hang up.

❑ DIALING A WRONG NUMBER

Everyone dials a wrong number at one time or another. You should know what to say when you hear an unfamiliar voice.

Don't ask, "Who is this?" Instead, ask for the person you are calling by name: "Is Maria there?" If you dialed the wrong number, the person on the other end will probably tell you there is no one named Maria there or simply that you have a wrong number. If you're not sure whether you dialed incorrectly or just have the wrong number, find out:

WRONG RESPONSE: "What number is this?" (There is no reason why the person you are talking to should give you his or her phone number. It's none of your business!)

RIGHT RESPONSE: "Is this 378-4269?" (By giving the

number you are dialing, you are not intruding on the person's privacy. If that person simply says "no," you will know for certain that you have misdialed.)

Before you hang up, make sure you apologize for bothering the person unnecessarily.

❏ Answering a Wrong Number

When the person calling you has dialed the wrong number, you should be understanding and patient, just as you would want someone else to be if you were in that spot. If the person asks what your phone number is, don't give it. Instead, ask what number the caller was trying to reach. If the phone number is different than yours, you can tell the person that he or she has misdialed.

❏ Talking to an Answering Machine

Many people feel uncomfortable talking to an answering machine. However, because so many individuals and businesses use these machines, everyone should get used to speaking to them.

It helps to imagine you are talking to the person you have called rather than to a machine. On the outgoing message, people usually specify whatever information they want you to leave. If they haven't asked for specific information, leave your name, your telephone number, the time and date you called (this is particularly helpful if the person you are calling is away on vacation or a trip), and a brief message explaining why you called.

Some answering machines only give you sixty seconds to leave your message, and then they automatically shut off. You should be prepared to say everything you need to in that amount of time. Otherwise, you may be cut off in mid-sentence and have to call back to leave the rest of your message. Don't rush through your message, however. Speak slowly and clearly so the person receiving the message will understand what you're saying when the message is played back.

Many answering machines now give the caller an unlimited time to speak and will state this in the announcement. Even with unlimited time, you should not talk forever, but be as brief as possible. Save the talk for when the person calls you back.

ANSWERING THE TELEPHONE

Most people answer the phone with a simple, "Hello." If you are at someone else's house, however, and answer the phone for that person, you might want to make it clear you don't live there. For example, you might answer, "The Johnson residence," so the caller will know that he or she has reached the right number, even though the voice answering is not familiar.

When you answer the phone at the place you work, you should be more businesslike and say the name of the business first and then your own name. For example: "Wanda's Gift Shop. Janet speaking. How may I help you?"

❑ WHEN YOU ARE HOME ALONE

When you are home alone and someone calls for a parent or other adult family member, for safety reasons it is not a good idea to tell whoever is calling that you are alone in the house. You basically have three options. You can simply not answer the phone; you can put on the answering machine; or you can answer the phone and make the person believe that someone else is home with you. Here are right and wrong ways to answer calls from people you don't know:

Caller: "Is your mother there?"

WRONG RESPONSE: "No, she's out shopping."

RIGHT RESPONSE: "Yes, but she's unable to come to the phone right now. May I take a message and she can call you back?"

If the person is someone you know, you may or may not want to reveal that your parents are not there with you. The choice is up to you.

If your family has an answering machine, you could turn the machine on and increase the volume so that you can hear who is leaving the message. This gives you the option of taking the call if it's someone you want to talk to or letting the person leave a message. Some people screen their calls this way all the time.

❏ TAKING MESSAGES

If you answer the phone and the person is calling someone who isn't home, always offer to take a message. Keep a pad of paper and a pencil or pen near all telephones so you don't waste time searching for these items. Write down the caller's name, phone number, and the reason for calling. If you miss something as you write, don't be afraid to ask the person to repeat the information. It's better to do that than to take down the wrong number or an incomplete message.

CHAPTER TWO
READING
ALOUD

Reading aloud to others, whether from a text written by you or by someone else, may appear at first glance to be the easiest form of public speaking. And in many ways it is. You don't have to think about what you're saying—the words are right there in front of you. All you have to do is read them. But it's not quite that easy.

To read well requires real effort. If you are reading a story or a poem, for example, you must convey the feelings of the writer to the people in your audience and hold their interest. That's no small achievement. Reading aloud is a skill, like any other kind of public speaking, and it requires practice.

By reading aloud, you get used to speaking to an audience. This is an excellent preparation for other forms of public speaking, where instead of reading you must speak for yourself.

Here are seven aspects of reading aloud that are important, regardless of what you are reading.

VOLUME

Speak up! You don't need to shout or strain, but project your voice enough so everyone in the room can hear you. Practice with a friend or family member in the largest room in your house. Can another person hear you if you read from the opposite end of the room? If not, you need to work on your volume. At first, you must be constantly aware of projecting your voice. With time, however, it will become second nature.

DICTION

Many people mumble or garble their speech or drop the endings of words when they read aloud. The best way to improve the clarity of your diction (the precise sounding of letters and words) is to practice. Exaggerate the pronunciation of each word clearly and distinctly. This exaggeration will make you aware of how important diction is and, again, will make speaking clearly second nature. You can also practice reading aloud into a tape recorder so that you can hear how you sound.

PRONUNCIATION

Often when you read, you might come across a word you either don't know the meaning of or can't pronounce. When you're reading silently to yourself, you can simply skip over the word; but you can't do that when you're reading aloud, without disrupting the flow and sense of what you are reading.

If you're reading a passage for the first time, you should try to pronounce the unfamiliar word as best you can. If you have mispronounced it, the teacher will usually come to your rescue. If you can't even begin to pronounce the word, don't be afraid to stop and simply say, "I'm not familiar with that word." Someone will help you out. You shouldn't feel bad

about not knowing the word. There are thousands of words in English, and most of us have a surprisingly limited vocabulary. Jot down the pronunciation and meaning of the word right away if you can, so you will be familiar with it next time you come across it.

PACE

Don't read too fast when you're reading aloud. You might be able to understand what you're reading, but your listeners will quickly be lost. Always read more slowly aloud than you would read silently to yourself. If you do, your listeners will be able to keep up with you, and you will be able to keep ahead of yourself by glancing ahead at the next sentence or phrase as you read.

Your reading rate should be about 120 to 185 words per minute. You can find out your reading rate by timing yourself as you read a passage that contains about 150 words. Use a stop watch or a regular or digital watch or clock. If you finished reading the passage in about one minute, your reading rate is good. If you finished it in less than one minute, you probably need to slow down.

BREATHING

Running out of breath in the middle of a sentence is one of the greatest fears that people have when they read aloud. To avoid this, try to take a deep breath at the end of every paragraph, which provides a natural break in all prose. Periods at the end of sentences and semicolons in the middle of sentences are perfect places to take a regular breath. Try to avoid taking a breath at a comma. The pause for a comma is normally too short for breathing.

VOCAL VARIETY

In normal conversation people don't talk to each other in a boring monotone, so there's no reason why you should read aloud in one. Try to vary the tone and pitch of your voice, no matter what it is you are reading. Don't always end a sentence by dropping or raising your voice; try both.

Put expression into your voice, particularly when reading a piece of imaginative literature. Match your vocal tone to the material whenever possible. For example, when reading a suspenseful story, create tension by slowly speeding up your reading as the story builds toward a climax.

POSTURE

Good posture will help you read and speak more effectively. Good posture keeps your vocal apparatus clear and open and allows you to project your voice without strain. Stand or sit erect when you read, with the book or paper up, not flat on the desk. Your head should not be looking down at the page. You should be poised but not rigid—being too rigid is almost as bad as being too relaxed.

FOUR KINDS OF MATERIAL TO READ ALOUD

Now let's look at four different kinds of texts you might be asked to read aloud in the classroom or to read to a younger brother or sister. Each type of reading presents its own set of challenges.

❑ READING FROM A TEXTBOOK

This is probably the most common kind of reading aloud you are asked to do in school. The teacher might ask you to read a passage from your textbook while the other students read along silently from their own books.

Whatever the subject—English, history, science, or math—it is your job to read the material clearly and make the passage as easy to understand and as interesting as possible. Because textbooks often contain lots of information, facts, and statistics, you may want to read these types of books a bit more slowly than you would read simpler material, so that your listeners can easily follow and absorb the information. Pause briefly between breaks in the text, such as headings, subheadings, and new chapters.

❑ READING A STORY

Storytelling is an old and respected art. The first stories weren't written down. They were told by professional storytellers, who handed them down orally from one generation to the next. Even when you are reading a written story, you are still telling it to others, many of whom are probably hearing it for the first time. Try to make the story come to life. Here are some tips on how to do it:

Read the story ahead of time if you can. If you know the plot and language of the story before you read it to your audience, you'll be better prepared to read it well. Try reading the story to yourself both silently and out loud.

Look at your audience. Of course while you're reading you're looking at the book or paper in front of you. But if you glance ahead at the next few words on the page, you can briefly raise your head and look out at the audience now and again. With practice, you can get quite good at this. Maintaining eye contact with members of the audience is important to keeping them interested in what you are saying. This is true in social and public speaking.

Read dialogue sections in the characters' voices. Dialogue refers to the words spoken directly by characters in fiction. They are set off by quotation marks. When you come to dialogue in a story, read it as the character speaking the words would say them, with expression. This adds drama and life to your reading. If more than one character is talking, vary your voice by changing the tone or raising or lowering pitch to make each character distinct from the others.

If the story has pictures, show them. If you are reading a picture book to younger children, make sure you pause to show—and even describe—the illustrations as you finish each page.

❏ READING A POEM

Poetry is the most compact and dense kind of creative literature. In a good poem, every word has importance—both for its sound and its meaning. Because of this, good diction and correct pronunciation of the words are critical.

The poet uses certain words in certain ways for their pleasing sounds. Alliteration is the repetition of the same initial letter, sound, or group of sounds in a series of words. For example, Edgar Allan Poe repeated the sounds of the letters *s* and *t* in this line from his poem "The Raven": "In there stepped a stately raven of the saintly days of yore."

Speaking Up in Class

Are you one of the first people to raise your hand when the teacher asks a question? Or are you one of the last? Speaking up in class is a form of public speaking that you probably face every day. How you offer an answer or response to a question often depends on how well you know the material and how confident you are about speaking up.

WHEN THE TEACHER ASKS A QUESTION

The most important aspect of volunteering in class is formulating an answer to the teacher's question. If you're shy about raising your hand and speaking out, answer the question in your head. If you're correct, you'll have given your confidence a boost and may find it easier to volunteer next time.

When you do raise your hand, hold it high, so the teacher can see it. Don't talk or make noises. You're more likely to be passed over for someone else who's better behaved. When answering the question, make sure you give a complete answer, preferably in the form of a sentence. For example, if the question is: "When did the Civil War begin?" Your answer will be clearer if you respond, "The Civil War began in 1861," and not simply "1861." You'll probably impress the teacher with your speaking skills, too.

No matter how anxious you are to get out the answer, speak slowly and clearly so you can be understood. Maintain eye contact with the teacher as you speak.

If your answer is incorrect, don't be discouraged. Everyone makes mistakes. Admit you were wrong and pay attention when the correct answer is given.

WHEN THE TEACHER CALLS ON YOU

When the teacher calls on you, you may or may not know the answer to the question. If you don't know the answer, say so. If you are unsure but think you might know it, take a chance. It's better to offer some answer than none at all. If you're wrong, don't feel bad. Listen for the correct answer and make a note of it. Remember, the more you volunteer in class, the less likely it is that you will be called on by the teacher when you don't know an answer. The ones who usually get called on are the students who never volunteer!

Assonance is the repetition of stressed vowel sounds in a series of words. John Greenleaf Whittier used *ow* and *ee* sounds in these lines from "Barbara Frietchie": "Round about them orchards sweep,/Apple and peach tree fruited deep."

Another important feature in poetry is meter, which is the arrangement of naturally accented and unaccented syllables in a line of poetry. The pattern of accents is often maintained throughout the poem. In these lines from Henry Wadsworth Longfellow's poem "Paul Revere's Ride," you can hear the natural rhythm created by the sounds of certain words and syllables: "Listen, my children, and you shall hear/Of the midnight ride of Paul Revere."

The meter of a poem creates a distinctive rhythm that should be emphasized by the reader. If possible, read the poem ahead of time, aloud and to yourself, to determine what the meter is and where to place accents.

Rhyme is another feature of most poetry. As you read poetry, you want to stress the rhymes without making the poem sound too sing-songy or predictable. Much contemporary poetry has little or no rhyme and can be read in a less formal, more conversational voice—Carl Sandburg's short poem "Fog," for example: "The fog comes/on little cat feet./It sits looking/over the harbor and city/on silent haunches/and then moves on."

Look for commas, hyphens, and other punctuation at the end of lines of poetry for cues when to pause while reading. Sometimes the thought or phrase continues on the next line, so you don't need to pause at all. Other times, even if there is no punctuation, you may need to pause to keep the meaning or phrasing of the line.

Before reading a poem aloud, it's a good idea to practice reading it to yourself at home, to discover what the meter is, where the rhymes, alliteration, and assonance occur, and to look up any unfamiliar words. You might borrow a record, tape, or CD from the library of a poet reading his or her own poetry. Listening to the way the poets interpret their own work will help you to read poetry with skill and expression.

❑ READING A PLAY

Most people think of plays as being performed on a theater stage. But there is a kind of play that is meant to be read without sets, costumes, lights, or action. This kind of performance is generally called reader's theater. In reader's theater, the actors sit in one place while reading their lines. The actors' voices stimulate the audience's imagination to fill in the missing details. The actors must read their parts with skill and expressiveness. Here are some hints on how to be a good and effective play reader:

Note stage directions. Stage directions are the words that aren't spoken by the actors in dialogue. They may be descriptions of action between speeches or words written in parentheses before a character's speech that denote emotion or feeling—for example, "with anger," "quietly," "sadly." Stage directions are cues that tell you how the character is feeling at that moment, and you should try to incorporate that feeling into your voice as you read the speech.

Understand your character. Every character in a well-written play has characteristics that make him or her unique. Look for clues about the character in what the person says and does. Understanding the personality and attitude of your character will help you to bring him or her convincingly to life.

Pay attention. It's easy to get lost in your own thoughts when it isn't your turn to read. But as a result, you may miss the cue for your next lines. This slows down the reading and disrupts the flow of the play. Read and listen carefully to the script so you won't hold things up.

Reading plays aloud can be fun and exciting. And play reading is a great introduction to the wonderful world of the theater.

Reading aloud may be the easiest form of public speaking, but like all public speaking, practice and experience will make it more interesting and rewarding—both for you and your audience.

KIDS SPEAK OUT: CAREERS AND SUCCESS

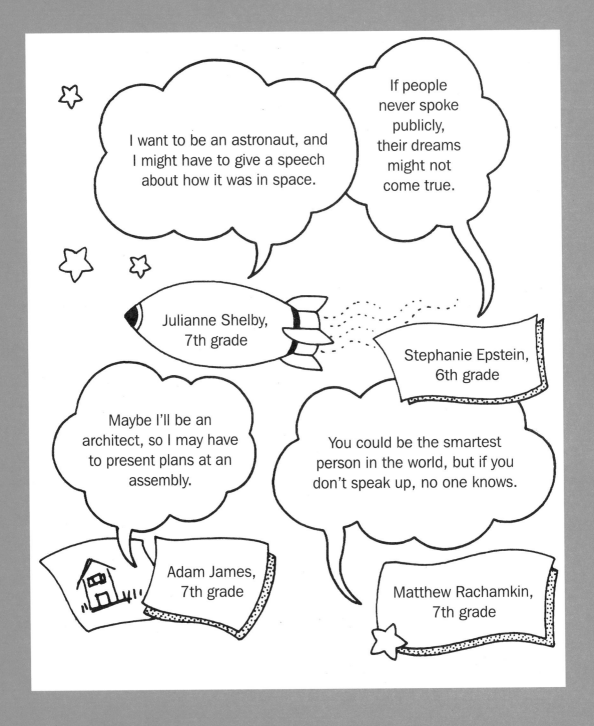

CHAPTER THREE
STAGE FRIGHT

AND HOW TO OVERCOME IT

It starts with a queasy feeling in the pit of your stomach. Sweat breaks out on your forehead, and your heart starts to pound. Your mouth is dry, and your mind is a blur. You try to concentrate on the words you are going to speak, but it's hopeless. You hear someone call your name, and you rise unsteadily to your feet. Your legs feel like they're made of rubber, and your hands are trembling. You wish with all your heart that you could be anywhere else in the world at this moment, even sitting in a dentist's chair as he prepares to drill. At least you wouldn't have to say anything, just open your mouth! You're sure the pain you would experience in the dentist's chair is slight compared with what you are feeling at this moment, one of the worst moments of your life.

Sound familiar? If you've ever had to speak to a large group of people, it may be. The symptoms described are part of a condition known as stage fright—extreme nervousness experienced by a speaker or actor.

Stage fright is perhaps the most serious problem faced by people who speak in public. That's why this entire chapter is devoted to it.

Before we examine ways to cope with stage fright, there are two important things you ought to know. The first is that *everyone* experiences stage fright at one time or another—adults as well as young people, experienced speakers as well as beginners. In one famous poll, people were asked what their greatest fears were. The number one answer given by the greatest number of people was having to speak before a large group. They said they were more afraid of that than of death itself! So you see, you are not alone.

The other thing you should know is that, believe it or not, nervousness before speaking publicly is natural and in many ways a good thing. We often get anxious and nervous before we do anything that we care

about, whether it's taking a big test in school or playing a game in a competitive sport. Nervousness keeps us on our toes, energizes us, and makes us aware of everything going on around us. A certain amount of nervousness is necessary to a good performance on the stage, on the playing field, or at the speaker's podium. Without feeling a little nervous, you would probably do a mediocre job. It is only when nervousness gets out of control that it becomes a problem.

To prevent a case of nerves from spilling over into a paralyzing case of stage fright, you should remember the two P's of public speaking—preparation and practice.

BE PREPARED

When you haven't planned your speech well and aren't sure what you're going to say, your natural fear and nervousness can turn into panic. On the other hand, the more prepared you are, the more likely it is that you will give an effective, successful speech. You'll be less likely to stumble over words as you speak, and you won't have to worry about what you're going to say next, because the words will be there when you need them. Thorough preparation is important to keeping your confidence high and your nervousness under control.

PRACTICE

Practice makes perfect. This old saying is as true when it comes to public speaking as it is in most other endeavors. Practice doesn't just mean practicing your speech in front of the mirror or before your parents or a good friend. It also means taking every opportunity that comes along to speak in public in order to get better at it. The more often you face an audience of listeners, the less fearful you will be of them. Good speakers are rarely born; they improve through experience.

As you practice and rehearse, you also keep improving the speech—both on the written page and in your delivery. Having other people watch and listen to you deliver your speech ahead of time also allows you to benefit from their constructive criticisms and advice.

SIX TECHNIQUES TO HELP YOU OVERCOME STAGE FRIGHT

These useful hints can help you calm down and get on with your speech.

❏ BREATHING

The way we breathe affects the way we speak. It also affects the way we feel. Just before you speak, take a few deep breaths. Hold the air in your lungs, count to five, and then release the breath slowly. This should relax you, calm your nerves, and steady you as you begin to speak. Continue to take slightly deep breaths as you speak to slow down your delivery and give you the breath you need to talk.

❏ RELAXATION

Breathing is just one way to relax your body. Another is to tense and then loosen the muscles in your arms, legs, and the rest of your body. Don't stand totally rigid at the podium. Notice whether or not your hands are tight; if they are, loosen them up. Be poised but relaxed. Relaxing your body will clear your mind and loosen your vocal cords, so that when you speak, the words will come out clearly and effectively.

❏ VISUALIZATION

The imagination can be a potent tool in overcoming stage fright. You can visualize a number of images to help calm yourself just before you begin speaking. Try several, and use the ones that work best for you.

One method is to close your eyes and visualize yourself speaking in a cool, confident manner with the audience hanging on your every word.

KiDs SpEaK OUt: HaNDLiNg StAgE fRiGHt

Another technique is to think of something you really enjoy doing and visualize yourself doing it. That can put you in a positive frame of mind as you start. Some speakers take the threat out of an audience by picturing them in their underwear! If you try this, however, be careful you don't break down with a bad case of the giggles!

❑ Focus

One thing that distracts many speakers is not knowing where to look while they are speaking. Some people fear that if they look into the audience, they may get stage fright and freeze up. These people might be more comfortable focusing on an object in the back of the room, but this tends to distance the speaker from the people he or she is talking to.

A better technique is to pick out a sympathetic face in the audience and focus on that person as you speak. You will feel as if you're talking to only this person, which will calm you and give your speech a feeling of intimacy. As you gain more experience, you might shift eye contact from one person or one group of people to another.

❏ Movement

One of the best ways to calm nerves and gain confidence when speaking is to move around. The very act of moving your body, or some part of it, will help break the spell of stage fright. Raise a hand as you speak, take a few steps away from the podium. Not only will the action make you feel better, but it will add drama and variety to your performance.

Your movements should be natural and not an extension of your nervousness (a tapping foot for example). They should also not be repeated too often. Too much movement will distract the audience from what you are saying.

❏ Concentration

Concentrate not on your words but on the ideas behind them. The words are the tools. They can be changed and shaped. The ideas that inspired the words are the important part of your speech. If you think about the ideas you want to get across, you will be less likely to forget what you are saying. You will be full of energy and excitement about your subject, and that enthusiasm should spread to your audience.

MISTAKES AND UNEXPECTED INTERRUPTIONS

All right, you say. You're well prepared, you've practiced your speech over and over, and you've tried several of the techniques described to calm your nerves. Then, right in the middle of your speech, your note cards fall on the floor. Or the principal delivers an announcement in a booming voice over the public-address system. Your whole speech falls apart, right?

Wrong! If you're prepared and practiced, these little things shouldn't throw you. If your note cards fall down, pick them up. If you make a mistake or stumble on a word, correct it and keep going. If a siren blares outside the window, stop talking until it fades away and then continue.

The worst thing you can do in one of these situations is to ignore the mistake or the interruption as if nothing happened. The audience knows something is wrong, so don't try to pretend there isn't. If you try to talk over the siren, you won't be heard. If you try to continue without your notes, you're likely to forget what you're saying. If you are distracted and need a moment to find your place again, that's okay. The audience will understand. They will sympathize with your problem and be supportive.

If after trying all these things, you are still nervous in front of an audience, the best thing to do may be to simply admit your fear. Prepare a little joke about your nervousness to open your speech with. Something like, "I'd rather be facing a firing squad right now, but the teacher says I have no choice." Your audience will probably chuckle and will understand your apprehension. It's something most of them can identify with! Also, by expressing your nervousness, you'll be able to get it out of the way. Then you can get on with your speech. It's important to remember that most audiences are ready and eager to listen to a speaker. The only thing that is holding you back from doing your job is your fear of failure. President Franklin Roosevelt once said, "The only thing we have to fear is fear itself." This is certainly true of stage fright. Once you face up to this irrational fear, you'll find public speaking isn't really all that difficult. In fact, it can be a very enjoyable and rewarding experience.

An oral report is an informative presentation of a topic made through speech. It will probably be one of the most frequent kinds of public speaking you will do in school. You may be asked to give an oral report on an event or person from American history, an aspect of science, a book you have read, or even a math topic.

Although presenting an oral report is similar to other kinds of public speaking, it is also different. Before you can begin to prepare your report, you must choose a topic and a purpose for it.

CHOOSING A TOPIC

Sometimes you will be assigned a topic for your oral report by your teacher. Other times you will be asked to choose your own. Keep these things in mind when choosing a topic.

The topic for your presentation should be:

Interesting to you. You should report on something you are really enthusiastic about. If you're excited by your topic, you'll probably do a good job researching and reporting on it, and your enthusiasm will spread to your audience.

The right length. Most classroom oral reports are between five and ten minutes long. If your topic is too broad, however, you won't be able to cover it sufficiently in that amount of time. If it is too narrow, you won't have enough to say about it. Broaden or narrow your topic to fit the time you have for your report.

For example, let's say you want to give an oral report on dinosaurs. If you try to talk about all kinds of dinosaurs, you would barely get started before your time would be up. If you choose just one type of dinosaur to talk about—such as the pterodactyl—you might not find enough information to fill the time period. Here's one way you might solve the problem. The pterodactyl is a type of flying dinosaur, or pterosaur. If you change your topic to pterosaurs, you could probably find enough information to fill the required time and cover the topic thoroughly.

Easily accessible. Make a preliminary visit to the school or public library to see how much information is available on your topic. If, for example, you can't find enough information on flying dinosaurs, you might consider choosing another topic—for example, meat-eating dinosaurs or dinosaurs that lived in water.

FOCUSING ON A PURPOSE

Every oral report must have a purpose or a reason. The three main purposes of oral reports usually are:

1. *to inform*—to give information about a topic: for example, education in colonial America, the life of your favorite rock singer;

2. *to persuade*—to express an opinion or belief on a topic and try to convince your audience to agree with you or take some action: for example, the importance of recycling, why the school year should be shorter;

3. *to entertain*—to give your audience an emotional experience through jokes, amusing or interesting stories (called anecdotes), and personal observations: for example, your life as a kid, your favorite pet.

The purpose of most oral reports you give in school will be to inform, but you may also want to keep the other two purposes in mind. While informing your listeners about an issue, such as crime, gun control, pollution, or AIDS, you may also want to persuade them to feel the way you do. If your report includes fascinating facts or anecdotes, you will be entertaining as well as informing the members of your audience. Even though your report may contain many features, be sure to keep your focus on your main purpose.

PREPARING YOUR ORAL REPORT

Now that you have chosen your topic and purpose, you are ready to begin preparing your report. The better prepared you are, the more confident you will be when making your presentation. And no matter how potentially good your report is, if you haven't prepared thoroughly, your presentation will not be effective.

Here are four important steps in preparing an oral report:

1. *Research your topic.* The library is the best place to start your research and may provide you with all the information you need. Look for information about your topic in books, reference works, newspapers, and other periodicals. Ask your librarian for help and keep your research notes organized in a notebook.

Don't overlook people as a source of information. Individuals who are experts, who have lived through a historical event, or who have a career related to your topic, are all good sources. (If your report is on a famous World War II battle, for example, you might interview your grandfather who was in the battle about his experiences.) Tape-record the interview so you'll be sure to get the person's exact words. You might even want to play part of the interview during your report, so your audience can hear the person's voice.

2. *Develop an outline.* An outline is the plan of a report. How you want to organize your outline and how detailed it will be is up to you. Most outlines include main points or ideas followed by supporting details, facts, and examples from your research notes.

3. *Write the report.* Use your outline as a guide, but change it as you are writing to fit your needs. Your draft does not have to be perfectly written. You can revise it later.

Creating
an Outline

An outline will help you plan your oral report. Organize the information from your research notes in a logical way so that your report flows smoothly.

Here is part of a sample outline on the life of talk-show host Oprah Winfrey:

A. Early Broadcast Career
   1. Became first black news anchorperson at Nashville TV station.
   2. Offered job at WJZ in Baltimore.
   3. Demoted from position as news anchor to local news reporter because of lack of "professionalism."
B. Success as Talk-Show Host
   1. Opportunity to co-host Baltimore morning show airing opposite *Phil Donahue Show.*
   2. Creation of her own talk-show program.
   3. Widespread popularity of her program presents her with other TV and film opportunities.

Your report should have a beginning (an introduction), a middle (a body), and an ending (a conclusion). The introduction should grab your audience's attention with an interesting fact, a rhetorical question, or perhaps a colorful quote from a famous person. (For example: "Oprah Winfrey is one of the most successful celebrities in America today. But when she was a teenager, it looked like she would never make it in life.")

The body of the report will contain the information in your outline—main ideas and supporting details. ("Oprah's big break came when she was asked to co-host a morning talk show in Baltimore that would air at the same time as the popular *Phil Donahue Show.*")

The conclusion will briefly summarize your report's main points and possibly reach some conclusion. ("Oprah continues to be one of the most popular people in the entertainment world. Talk-show host, actress, producer, spokesperson on issues she cares about—Oprah has done it all.")

4. *Think about adding audio and visual aids.* Audio and visual aids are extra elements that appeal to the ear and eye. They may include charts, pictures, videos, audiocassettes, and CDs. They can add color and variety to your report and make it clearer and more intelligible to your audience.

THE BEST WAY TO PRESENT YOUR REPORT

There are three ways you can deliver your report. You can read it, memorize it, or improvise it. Each of these ways has its advantages and disadvantages:

❏ READING YOUR REPORT

At first, this may seem the easiest and safest way to deliver your report. There's little or no chance that you'll forget something or suffer stage fright. It seems guaranteed that you'll say exactly what you want to say and use the right words to express yourself. But there are some major disadvantages:

Reading can be boring to listen to. When we read, our speech tends to be less expressive, less animated, and less interesting. You'll run the risk of losing your audience's attention.

It's difficult to make eye contact. Instead of looking out at your audience, your eyes will most likely be glued to the page. If you try to look up, you may lose your place as you read.

It will be difficult to use audiovisual aids. If you are reading your report, you may have to stop while you start the projector or the tape cassette and find your place again. To avoid this awkward problem, you may decide simply to drop all audio and visual aids from your report, which might make your presentation less informative and even less interesting.

You should not read your report, unless reading is part of your assignment or you are so terrified of public speaking that it is the only way you can deliver the report.

❑ MEMORIZING YOUR REPORT

This may seem the ideal way to make your presentation. If you know every word by heart, you can keep your eyes on your audience and move about freely. However, memorizing is hard work and will take you lots of time—time that might be better spent on improving your report in other ways. Also, there is a very good chance that you will go blank at some point, forget what you were going to say next, and panic. Then your well-planned report will turn into a first-class disaster.

❑ IMPROVISING YOUR REPORT WITH NOTES

This is the best way to deliver your report and most other kinds of public speeches. It is a compromise between memorization and reading aloud. With this method, you have written notes that you can refer to as you speak, but you also know your material well enough that you don't have to rely on them every second. You can maintain eye contact with the audience, move around freely, and deal confidently with audiovisual aids. Most important of all, because you aren't working from a set script, your report will sound more natural and conversational in tone. You will be talking to your audience, not reading or lecturing to them.

Here are some steps to follow as you prepare an improvised report:

Write your notes on 3 x 5 file cards. These are easy to handle, compact, and will fit into the palm of your hand. Make sure they are numbered and stacked in the proper order.

Keep notes brief and to the point. Use your notes as written cues, not as text to be read. You should know your topic well enough that a word or phrase will prompt you to recall the information you want to share. However, you may want to write out your entire introduction, especially if it includes an anecdote or a quotation. You may also want to write out the conclusion, so that you'll be sure to summarize everything you have said as briefly and clearly as possible.

Practice, practice, practice! To get your delivery down pat, practice your speech in front of a mirror. Keep track of the time with a stopwatch or a timer. If your report is too long, edit out some details. If it is too short, add more details or another main point. (For example, in your report on Oprah Winfrey, eliminate or add facts about Oprah's television program or her work in films.)

Work on eye contact, appearance, and gestures. When you feel more confident, present your oral report to close friends or family members. Have them critique you and suggest ways in which you might improve your performance. If possible, record your presentation on an audiocassette recorder or video camera. Examine the tape carefully for ways to improve your delivery, diction, and posture.

Writing Your Speech Notes From an Outline

An outline is a brief framework for your oral report. When you write your notes on file cards, you will probably want to be even briefer. One word or phrase should be enough to trigger your memory of what you want to say.

This is part of a note card based on the sample outline for the report on Oprah Winfrey:

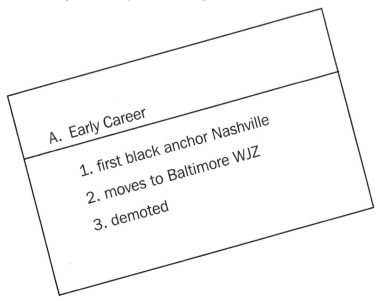

A. Early Career

    1. first black anchor Nashville

    2. moves to Baltimore WJZ

    3. demoted

AUDIOVISUAL AIDS

Audio and visual aids come in many shapes and sizes. As shown in the box at right, each type of aid is best at illustrating particular types of information.

Here are some general rules to follow when using any kind of audiovisual aid:

Be sure you know how to operate the equipment. Don't wait until you are beginning your report to find out how to operate the overhead projector or the VCR. Any fumbling you do wastes time and frustrates you and your audience.

Plan when you will use the aid. Make sure you show the aid as you are referring to the information or point that it illustrates. If you show it before or after, you will confuse your audience.

TYPE OF VISUAL OR AUDIO AID	AN EFFECTIVE WAY TO:
Graphs and Charts	present statistics; compare information
Pictures, Photographs, Slides	make a point visually; personalize an issue or person; create emotional response in an audience
Diagrams and Models	show the parts or working of something technical or mechanical
Filmstrips, Movies, Videotapes	supplement or illustrate information; add excitement, color, and interest
Audiocassettes and CDs	present examples of music, sounds (animals, birds, nature), or the words and voices of people
Flip Charts	present a combination of words and images; present sequential information
Chalkboard	write words and phrases for emphasis

Point out important details. If you are using a projected image, flip chart, or other visual aid, focus on what information you want the audience to see with your finger or, even better, with a pointer.

Don't block the view. A visual aid is useless if people can't see it. Step back so that everyone in the room will have a clear view.

Don't talk to the visual aid. There's a tendency among speakers to look at the screen or chalkboard and not at the audience. Avoid doing this—it takes your focus off the audience and if you're talking they won't be able to hear you. So don't talk while writing on the chalkboard, and whenever you need to turn away, turn back to face your audience as quickly as possible.

Know your space. If possible, check out the room ahead of time. Be sure you know where the light switches are and how to shut the blinds if you need to darken the room for a filmstrip or movie. Stand in the back of the room and see if any charts and pictures will be clearly visible. If not, enlarge them on a copy machine or find a better visual aid. Nothing's more frustrating for an audience than not being able to see a visual aid that is being referred to by the speaker.

Move quickly. Refer to the aid when you need to, then put it away and get on with your report. About thirty seconds is usually enough time for the audience to absorb the information shown in a visual aid.

Don't overdo it. Too many audio and visual aids will clutter your presentation and detract from what you have to say. Choose a few good ones as departure points for discussion and not as ends in themselves.

PRESENTING YOUR REPORT: A LAST-MINUTE CHECKLIST

You're prepared and practiced and ready to go. Before you begin, ask yourself these questions:

- Do I have everything I need, including note cards and visual aids?
- Have I checked to make sure all the equipment I will be using is in working order?
- Have I allowed myself enough time to look over the room and set up my things?
- Have I reviewed my notes one last time?
- Is my appearance neat and my hair combed?
- Are my clothes a little nicer than what I might normally wear to school?
- Is my attitude positive and my energy level high?
- Is my body relaxed?

As you give your oral report, keep these "Four B's" in mind:

Be comfortable. If you're relaxed, your audience will be, too. If you're tense, you will communicate that to your audience, and they will be uncomfortable, too. Relax your body. Stand erect but not stiff. Move around a little if you need to. Hang loose.

Be yourself. Don't think of this presentation as a lecture or a formal talk. You're sharing something with a group of friends. Be conversational, casual, and personal. Don't put on false airs. Remember—you're not the teacher!

Be enthusiastic. You chose this topic because you were excited about it. Now it's time to transfer that excitement to your audience. If you're energized and enthusiastic, they will sit up and listen. If you're bored, they will be, too.

Be confident. You've prepared and practiced. You know your topic forward and backward. So take charge and enjoy your moment in the spotlight!

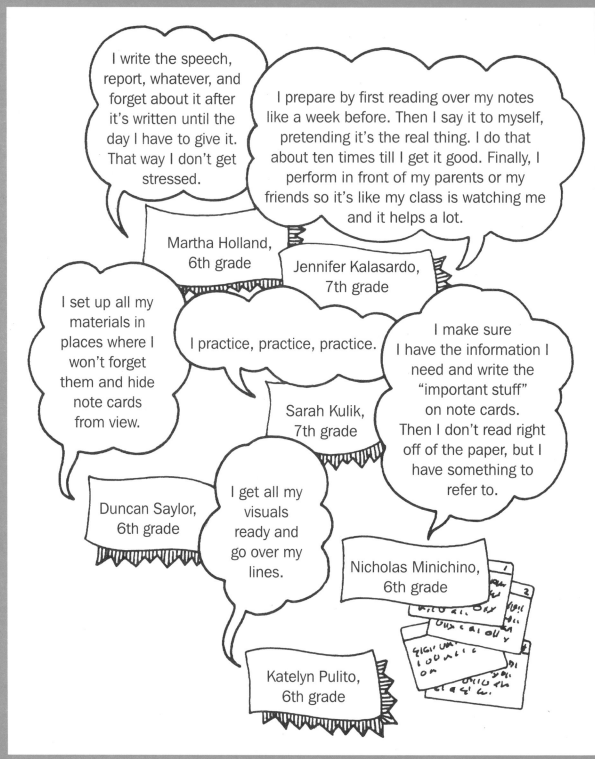

ORAL PRESENTATIONS

An oral presentation is a less detailed report than an oral report, and it is usually about a single idea or process. It may describe how something works, for example, or it may be the telling of a story or reenacting of a folktale or legend.

Here are some examples of topics for oral presentation:

- demonstrating how the invention you made for the science fair works
- describing a picture or poster you made in art class and what it means
- performing a magic trick
- explaining how a game or other activity is played
- describing a craft or other hobby or activity
- telling a story or folktale by acting it out with a partner

An oral presentation differs from an oral report in some other important ways. While a report is usually given in a classroom to a group of students, an oral presentation may not be. It might be given during a science fair, for example, or an open house for parents when many people will be looking at your presentation in small groups. In some cases, you may have to repeat your presentation many times. You will have to know how to operate any equipment or moving parts and practice using them.

Here are a few more hints for giving an oral presentation:

Talk loudly and clearly. This is important because other activities and noises may be going on around you, distracting your listeners.

Keep it simple. Your demonstration should not be unnecessarily long or complicated, even if the process you are describing is. Leave out any details that are unnecessary and could confuse the listener. Break down the process into a series of steps and write notes for each step on file cards that you can refer to as you speak. Step-by-step illustrations may also be helpful visual aids.

Use sequential words to describe a process. The words "first," "second," "next," "then," and "finally" all help make the steps in a sequence of events clear and understandable.

Be prepared to answer questions. When listening to a presentation, people often ask questions about things they don't understand or want to know more about. Be prepared to answer these questions by knowing the subject of your presentation as thoroughly as possible. If you don't know the answer to a question, don't make up an answer. Be honest and admit that you don't know.

CHAPTER FIVE

SPEECHES FOR EVERY OCCASION

"Speech! Speech!"

You've heard this familiar cry from the crowd at a banquet or other grand occasion in movies, books, or your imagination. A distinguished-looking man or woman rises from a chair, smiles at the audience, speaks eloquently for fifteen minutes and, after a moment of silence, sits down to thunderous applause.

A speech is a formal talk given on a special occasion. A successful speech is the crowning moment of public speaking. Great speeches have changed the course of history, moved people to change their lives, transformed ordinary men and women into heroes, and expressed the feelings and aspirations of whole peoples and nations. Think of Abraham Lincoln's Gettysburg Address, John F. Kennedy's inaugural address, or Martin Luther King, Jr.'s "I have a dream" speech during the civil rights march on Washington in 1963.

There is something self-important and momentous about such famous speeches that frightens ordinary people from ever wanting to give one. However, it shouldn't.

Many of the details and steps of preparing and giving a speech are similar to those for an oral report. In both cases, you need to focus on a topic and a purpose, take similar steps to prepare (make notes, an outline), use audiovisual aids when appropriate, and be aware of your appearance, posture, and diction. Many speeches, like most oral reports, are improvised, using note cards. Some speeches, particularly political speeches and those with a serious theme, however, may be read.

Being able to write a good speech and deliver it convincingly is an important skill. Good speakers make strong leaders. Being able to organize your ideas and communicate them to others is a life skill that will be useful in whatever career you pursue.

THE KEY TO SPEECHMAKING: KNOW YOUR AUDIENCE

Although purpose is important when creating a speech, it's equally important to know the audience you are speaking to. The audience for most of your oral reports and presentations is probably made up of your classmates, but the audience for a speech may vary greatly. The audience may be composed of adults, children your own age, or members of an organization or sports team you are a member of.

How you shape your speech, the tone you give it, and even the topic you choose, will depend very much on who your audience is and what interests them. You probably wouldn't chose to talk about the joys of iron welding to the local chapter of the Great Books Club. Nor would you tell a silly school joke to a group of adults. By tailoring your speech to your audience, you will be assured that they will listen with interest and that your speech will be a success.

You may think that as a young person you will not have much occasion to give a speech. But that isn't true. Here are four kinds of speeches that you might find yourself asked to give and some pointers on how you might best rise to each occasion.

THE CAMPAIGN SPEECH

"If elected I will...." These words have become a cliché, as have other phrases associated with speeches by people running for public office. But campaign speeches serve a serious purpose. They offer the voters a chance to hear and see the candidates and find out where they stand on important issues. If you run for class president, student council, or another office in school or a club you belong to, you may be required to give a short campaign speech. Here are some pointers to keep in mind when preparing a campaign speech:

Be fresh and original. Too many campaign speeches sound alike. The speaker trots out the same tired old phrases that voters have heard time and again. To set yourself off from the other candidates, be different. Open with a startling fact or a funny story that pertains to your campaign. (For example, "I've been running for years on the baseball field, the soccer field, and the football field. Now I figure it is time to run on the political field as your student council president.")

Get specific. Don't talk in generalities. Tell exactly what you'll do to improve things if elected. Find an issue that you and your audience care about. (For example, "Everyone complains about the cafeteria food. If I'm elected student council president, I promise to set up a meeting with the principal and the cook to work toward more varied menus and better food.") Come up with a workable solution to a problem that you think you can realistically achieve. But don't make promises you can't keep.

Give your credentials. Experience is an important qualification for any elective office. If you have any experience that relates to the job, make sure you state it in your speech. Give your academic record, years at the school or in the organization, other responsibilities, and extracurricular activities you've been involved in. Explain how this experience makes you an ideal candidate. If, for example, you have served as captain of a sports team or a club officer, you have valuable leadership experience to bring to the position you are running for. Even mention part-time jobs if they're relevant. Maybe you worked a cash register at a store last summer and have experience handling money, a good qualification for class treasurer.

Don't put down the competition. Some politicians think that knocking the other candidates is the way to win, but negative campaigning often has a way of boomeranging on the person who's doing it. Mean-spirited attacks make you look bad and could hurt in the polls. Instead, be positive, build yourself up without tearing down others.

Keep it short. Less is usually better. This is a rule for many kinds of speeches. Hit your main points, entertain and inform your audience, summarize what you have said, and get off. A long, rambling speech could irritate your listeners and actually lose you votes.

THE ACCEPTANCE SPEECH

Okay. Your campaign speech was great, and it helped you win the election. Now you must make an acceptance speech. Or maybe you have won an award or are being recognized for some special achievement. An acceptance speech, like a campaign speech, has one overriding purpose—to accept graciously.

Here are three B's to keep in mind when formulating your acceptance speech:

Be appreciative. You earned the award or position, but it was through the help of other people. Thank them for their support and belief in you and in your abilities. Mention individuals by name who were particularly helpful or supportive.

Be brief. Don't give a long list of names of people you want to thank. Just thank the most important people. Remember those celebrities at the Academy Awards who get cut off by the orchestra because they talk too long. Brevity is particularly important if people other than you are being recognized at the same event. Leave some time for them to have their say, too.

Be generous. The only thing worse than a poor loser is a mean-spirited winner. Mention, and even compliment, those who competed with you for this honor. It will make them feel better and will make you look better. And remember, next time you might be sitting where they are!

THE PUBLIC MEETING SPEECH

Communities often hold public hearings or town meetings to discuss or vote on important issues that affect the community. The issue might be the development of a new shopping center down the street, the installation of a traffic light on a busy street corner, or the need for a youth center. Individuals who feel strongly for or against the issue are invited to stand up and speak their piece.

If the issue is something that you care about, you might want to attend with your parents and even decide to speak out yourself. This kind of speech is one of the most important you may ever be asked to deliver. What you say at a public hearing could influence other people and help shape a final decision.

This kind of speech should be short and to the point. Many people may be speaking, and you must make your points quickly and accurately. You may want to have your speech written out on file cards. Or you may want to write down your major points so you don't forget them.

Here are a few other hints to help you make your speech effective:

Keep your emotions in check. Feelings often run strong on a controversial issue. Don't let your emotions run away with you. Let your feelings strengthen your speech, but don't let them get out of hand. By keeping cool and reasonable, you will influence more listeners and deliver your speech more effectively.

Be positive. No matter how strongly you feel for or against the issue, don't brand your opponents as devils. Try to be positive in your criticism and don't turn a public issue into a personal vendetta.

Focus on the public. Perhaps the issue affects you personally, but that should not be the focus of your argument. Show how the entire neighborhood or community is affected by this issue. If you do this, no one will ignore what you have to say as self-serving and criticize you for only looking out for your own interests.

WHEN THE SPOTLIGHT ISN'T ON YOU: INTRODUCTORY SPEECHES

There are occasions when you may speak in a supporting capacity—either to introduce a main speaker at an event or to give an award or recognition to a special person. Being an introductory speaker is a good way to break into public speaking. It gets you used to speaking before a group, yet the speech itself is short. Like acceptance speeches, introductory speeches should be brief—usually a minute or two is long enough.

Here are three things you should include when you are making a speech to introduce another person:

The person's name. If you don't know the person very well, make sure you know the correct pronunciation of his or her name. This is not the time to get it wrong!

The person's qualities. Briefly describe two or three characteristics or achievements that qualify the person for this award. Be sincere but be brief.

The name of the award or the topic of the speech. If there is an inscription on the award or trophy, read it. If the person is giving a speech, mention briefly what the topic will be. Leave the rest to the speaker.

If the person is getting an award, make sure you let everyone see it clearly. Once you have introduced the person, shake his or her hand. Then get out of the way and let that person have the spotlight.

❏ RECOGNIZING OR AWARDING A GROUP OF PEOPLE

You may be asked at a school assembly to recognize a group of people who are receiving awards. Again, you will want to review the list of names beforehand and make sure you can pronounce each name correctly. Give each person time to get up on stage to receive the award before reading the next name. If this isn't possible due to time restraints or the number of people, read the names at a measured pace, so you don't fall too far behind or ahead of the people being honored. Pause if there is any applause after you say each person's name.

Chairing
a Meeting

A meeting is as much a public occasion as an assembly or a dinner. It might be a meeting of a school organization or a social group that you belong to outside of school. Whatever the group, the chairperson is the one who conducts the meeting and sees that it runs smoothly. The chairperson also makes sure that all business is attended to and that everyone gets the opportunity to speak. Being a chairperson is more like being the conductor of an orchestra than a person giving a speech, but the job is public speaking just the same.

Chairing a meeting, whether it's one time or on a regular basis, can be rewarding. It's fun being in charge of something.

Many adult chairpersons follow a format for a meeting called parliamentary procedure. You may find that the six basic steps of parliamentary procedure provide a good framework for conducting your meeting:

1. The call to order. This simply means that you get everyone quieted down and the meeting started. You probably won't do this until everyone who is supposed to be there is present. This is also a good time to introduce any guests at the meeting or new members of your group.

2. Reading of minutes of last meeting. The minutes are the description of highlights of the last meeting and are usually recorded and read aloud by the secretary. If your group doesn't keep minutes, you may want to informally review what took place at the last meeting, if it relates to the present meeting.

3. Reports from committees and individuals. This is the meat-and-potatoes part of the meeting. People who have business to report do so, one at a time. It is your job as the chairperson to call on each person and field any questions from other members.

4. Old business. This includes any topics or items left unfinished at the last meeting. As chairperson, you moderate the discussion and see that it is conducted in an orderly fashion.

5. New business. As with old business, you moderate the discussion and see that it is conducted in an orderly fashion.

6. Adjournment. This means calling an end to the meeting. Before you do so, you will probably want to schedule the next meeting and make sure the group members have their assignments and responsibilities for that meeting.

THE IMPROMPTU SPEECH

An impromptu speech is one that is given on the spur of the moment with little or no preparation. For people who are fearful of public speaking, this is probably the most frightening speech of all. Just imagine. You are attending your friend's birthday party or a sports award dinner, and just before it begins, the person in charge asks you to prepare a few words to say because the person who was going to speak got sick at the last minute.

Before you say you are beginning to feel sick yourself, or have developed a sudden case of laryngitis, consider this. If you have attained some experience as a public speaker—by giving oral reports or presentations, for example—an impromptu speech should not be such a daunting proposition. If you are asked to introduce someone or give an award, you can rely on what you already know about speaking to an audience and simply get the information you need to make the presentation. If you are asked to speak on a topic you know something about, you should be able to take your prior knowledge and, in a short time, structure a brief speech with an opening, a middle, and a conclusion.

Perhaps the best thing about giving an impromptu speech is that you don't have the time to worry about it. When you have days or weeks to prepare a speech, you have lots of time to worry and fret. When you only have a short time to prepare, you can't stop to worry too much. You just get up and do it. Finally, an impromptu speech should never be very long, so no matter how bad it may seem, just remember, it'll be over quickly.

When you have given a successful impromptu speech, you have conquered the last challenge of public speaking. When you can speak well on such short notice, you can do just about anything.

KIDS SPEAK OUT: TOPICS FOR IMPROMPTU SPEECHES

For Future Reference: Toastmaster and After-Dinner Speaker

These are two kinds of speechmaking you may never have to perform or, if you do, it will be when you are much older. But it may be a good idea to know what these speaking roles are and what is expected of the speaker on each occasion.

A toastmaster is a person who conducts a banquet or dinner in much the same manner that a chairperson conducts a meeting. As the name implies, the toastmaster's first task is to propose toasts. A toast is a statement in honor of a person, group, or sentiment that people at a gathering raise their glasses and drink to. The toastmaster also acknowledges persons in the room, tells jokes and anecdotes, and generally sees that the evening's program runs smoothly and on time. Being a toastmaster requires the skill of a seasoned public speaker who knows how to speak and introduce people with confidence and style.

After-dinner speakers are also highly experienced public speakers. When groups or organizations meet for a monthly or annual meal (it may be breakfast or lunch instead of dinner), they often invite a speaker to provide an entertaining half-hour talk when the meal is over. The key word here is entertaining. The after-dinner speaker may inform or persuade, but his or her central purpose is to entertain and amuse. The pace is relaxed and conversational. A good after-dinner speaker has a large supply of jokes and funny stories to tell his or her audience. After-dinner speakers are often in high demand and are usually paid for their services.

You may never be a toastmaster or an after-dinner speaker, but if you truly enjoy public speaking and have a knack for putting people at ease, you may consider giving this a try.

BUILDING UP YOUR REPERTOIRE: CREATE A SPEECH FILE

Whatever kind of speech you are giving, it's a good idea to be prepared. By having tools at hand, you can prepare a speech for a particular audience or on a particular topic more quickly and effectively. One way to do this is to start a speech file. Here are some of the things you might put into your file:

- Clippings from newspapers and magazines that relate to topics or give you ideas for speeches. They also might contain interesting or unusual quotations, facts, or statistics that you could use in a speech.
- Ideas from personal experiences that have happened to you or to friends or family members. An interesting anecdote might be the perfect illustration for your speech and give it a warm and personal touch that will win over your audience.

In addition to your speech file, start a reference shelf of books that include the following:

- Almanacs and other fact books. For information and statistics to give your speech a good opening or a new insight. Some good ones are *The People's Almanac, The Universal Almanac,* and *The Information Please Almanac.*
- Quotation books. The most popular and best known of these is *Bartlett's Familiar Quotations,* but there are many others. The quotations are usually organized by topics. A good quote from a famous person may make an attention-grabbing, and thought-provoking opening for your speech.
- Joke books. A good joke or funny story can illustrate a point in a way that people remember. It can also start your speech off on the right foot. Many joke books organize the jokes by topic for easy reference.

acceptance speech—A brief speech a person gives when receiving an award or other honor.

after-dinner speaker—A person who delivers an entertaining speech following a formal dinner or banquet.

alliteration—A poetic device in which the poet repeats the same initial letter, sound, or group of sounds in a series of words.

anecdote—A short, usually amusing, story used to illustrate a point.

assonance—A poetic device in which stressed vowel sounds are repeated in a series of words.

audiovisual aids—Elements that appeal to the ear or eye in a speech and that provide information or illustrate a point. Examples include charts, pictures, videos, audiocassettes, and CDs.

campaign speech—A speech given by someone running for public office.

chairperson—The person who conducts a meeting and sees that it runs smoothly.

dialogue—The words spoken directly by characters in fiction or plays.

diction—Clearness in speaking and the pronunciation of words.

impromptu speech—A speech given on the spur of the moment with little or no preparation.

introductory speech—A brief speech given to introduce another person.

meter—The arrangement of accented and unaccented syllables in a line of poetry.

minutes—The description of the highlights of a meeting, usually recorded and read by the secretary.

oral presentation—A focused talk on a particular subject, usually narrower in scope than an oral report and often involving the description or explanation of how something works or how a process functions.

oral report—A detailed and informative spoken presentation of a topic.

parliamentary procedure—An official set of rules for conducting formal meetings of groups or organizations.

public or town meeting—A meeting held to hear citizens' opinions and feelings on community issues.

public speaking—Speaking to a group of people in a public setting with a purpose.

reader's theater—A style of theater in which the actors read plays for an audience of listeners without sets, costumes, lights, or action.

speech—A formal talk given on a special occasion.

stage directions—The description of the action of a play or of emotions of a character who is speaking.

stage fright—Extreme nervousness experienced by a speaker or actor before an audience.

toast—A statement in honor of a person, group, or sentiment that people at a gathering raise their glasses and drink to.

toastmaster—A person at a banquet or dinner whose job is to lead the toasts, tell jokes and anecdotes, and see that the program runs smoothly.

Berry, Michele. *Help Is on the Way for: Oral Reports* (Chicago: Childrens Press, 1986.)

Detz, Joan. *You Mean I Have to Stand Up and Say Something?* (New York: Macmillan, 1986.)

Gilbert, Sara. *You Can Speak Up in Class* (New York: Morrow Junior Books, 1991.)

Gilford, Henry. *How to Give a Speech* (New York: Franklin Watts, 1980.)

Ryan, Margaret. *So You Have to Give a Speech* (New York: Franklin Watts, 1987.)

Sternberg, Patricia. *Speak Up! A Guide to Public Speaking* (New York: Julian Messner, 1984.)

Steven Otfinoski, of Stratford, Connecticut, has published numerous children's books, mysteries, and biographies. He is the author of *Boris Yeltsin and the Rebirth of Russia, Joseph Stalin: Russia's Last Czar,* and *Nelson Mandela: The Fight Against Apartheid,* also published by The Millbrook Press.